Symbols of U.S. State Flags Coloring Book

Kreativ Entspannen

Kreativ Entspannen

COLORING / ACTIVITY BOOKS FOR ADULTS

Copyright 2016

ALABAMA

This is a Bleed Through Page If You Are Using a Coloring Marker or Pen!
Find Other Great Titles By searching for Kreativ Entspannen on Your Favorite Book Retailer
Amazon.Com | Barnes & Noble (BN.Com) | Books A Million (BAM.Com)

Kreativ Entspannen

COLORING / ACTIVITY BOOKS FOR ADULTS

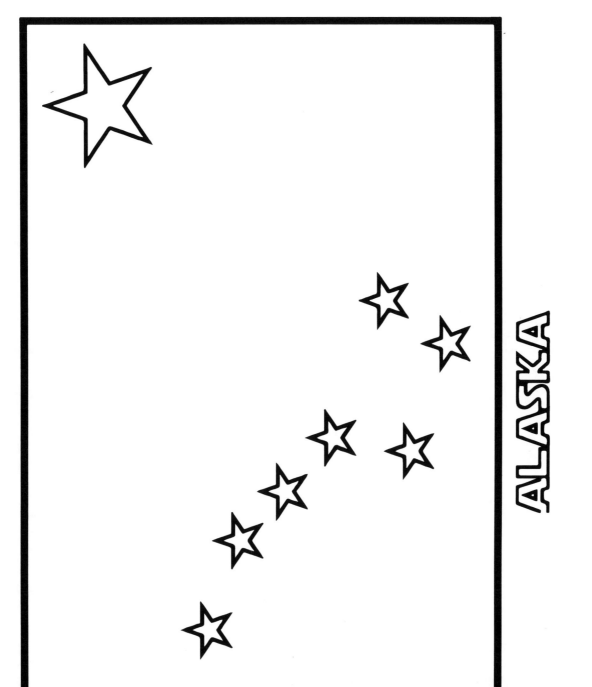

ALASKA

ARIZONA

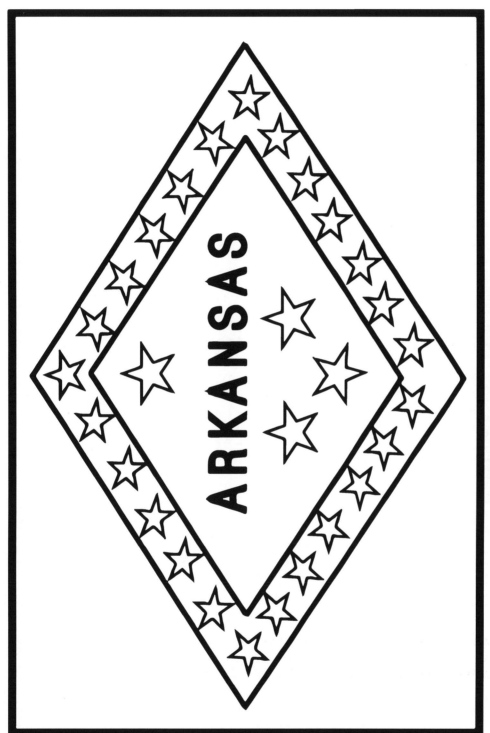

ARKANSAS

CALIFORNIA REPUBLIC

CALIFORNIA

This is a Bleed Through Page If You Are Using a Coloring Marker or Pen!
Find Other Great Titles By searching for Kreativ Entspannen on Your Favorite Book Retailer
Amazon.Com | Barnes & Noble (BN.Com) | Books A Million (BAM.Com)

Kreativ Entspannen

COLORING / ACTIVITY BOOKS FOR ADULTS

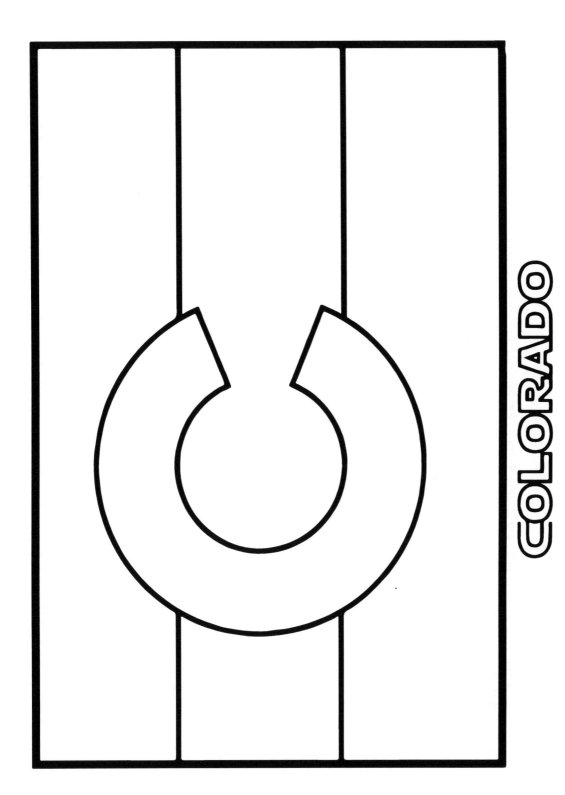

COLORADO

CONNECTICUT

FLORIDA

This is a Bleed Through Page If You Are Using a Coloring Marker or Pen!
Find Other Great Titles By searching for Kreativ Entspannen on Your Favorite Book Retailer
Amazon.Com | Barnes & Noble (BN.Com) | Books A Million (BAM.Com)

Kreativ Entspannen

COLORING / ACTIVITY BOOKS FOR ADULTS

GEORGIA

HAWAII

IDAHO

ILLINOIS

ILLINOIS

INDIANA

DECEMBER 7, 1787

DELAWARE

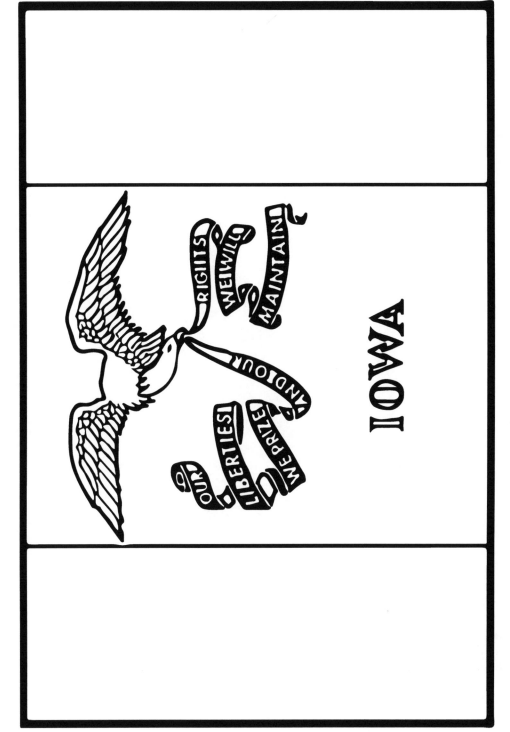

IOWA

This is a Bleed Through Page If You Are Using a Coloring Marker or Pen!
Find Other Great Titles By searching for Kreativ Entspannen on Your Favorite Book Retailer
Amazon.Com | Barnes & Noble (BN.Com) | Books A Million (BAM.Com)

Kreativ Entspannen

COLORING / ACTIVITY BOOKS FOR ADULTS

KANSAS

KANSAS

KENTUCKY

LOUISIANA

This is a Bleed Through Page If You Are Using a Coloring Marker or Pen!
Find Other Great Titles By searching for Kreativ Entspannen on Your Favorite Book Retailer
Amazon.Com | Barnes & Noble (BN.Com) | Books A Million (BAM.Com)

Kreativ Entspannen

COLORING / ACTIVITY BOOKS FOR ADULTS

MAINE

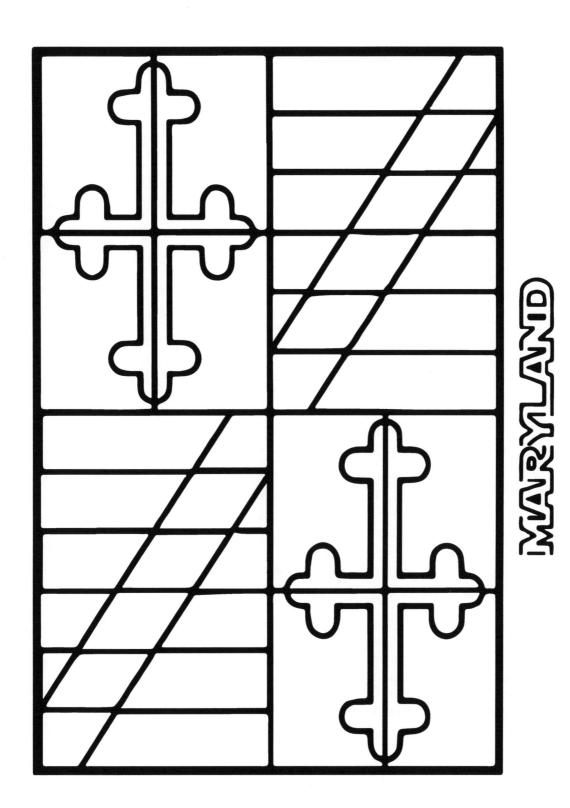

MARYLAND

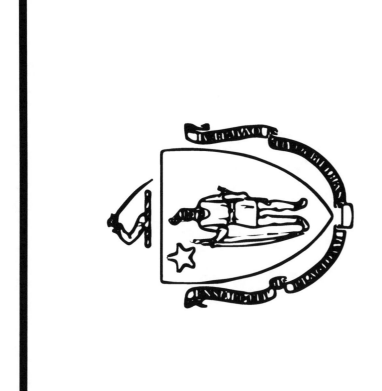

MASSACHUSETTS

MICHIGAN

MINNESOTA

MISSISSIPPI

MISSOURI

MONTANA

MONTANA

NEBRASKA

This is a Bleed Through Page If You Are Using a Coloring Marker or Pen!
Find Other Great Titles By searching for Kreativ Entspannen on Your Favorite Book Retailer
Amazon.Com | Barnes & Noble (BN.Com) | Books A Million (BAM.Com)

Kreativ Entspannen

COLORING / ACTIVITY BOOKS FOR ADULTS

NEVADA

This is a Bleed Through Page If You Are Using a Coloring Marker or Pen!
Find Other Great Titles By searching for Kreativ Entspannen on Your Favorite Book Retailer
Amazon.Com | Barnes & Noble (BN.Com) | Books A Million (BAM.Com)

Kreativ Entspannen

COLORING / ACTIVITY BOOKS FOR ADULTS

NEW HAMPSHIRE

NEW JERSEY

NEW MEXICO

NEW YORK

NORTH CAROLINA

NORTH DAKOTA

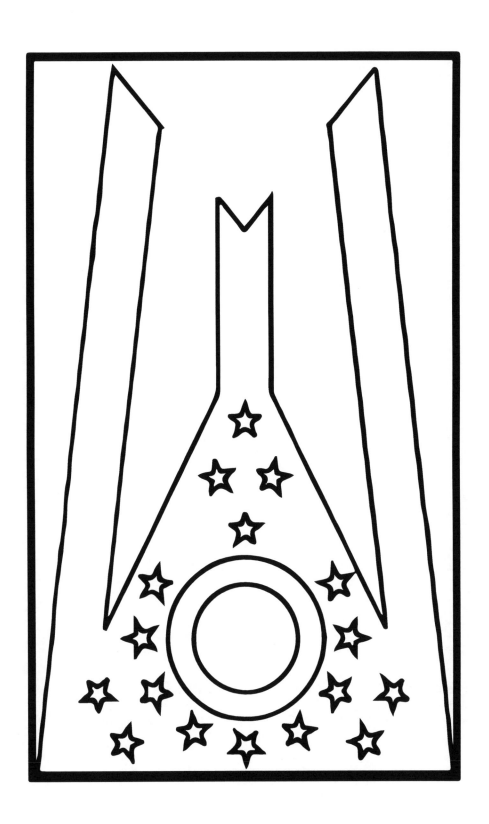

OHIO

OKLAHOMA

OKLAHOMA

STATE OF OREGON

1859

OREGON

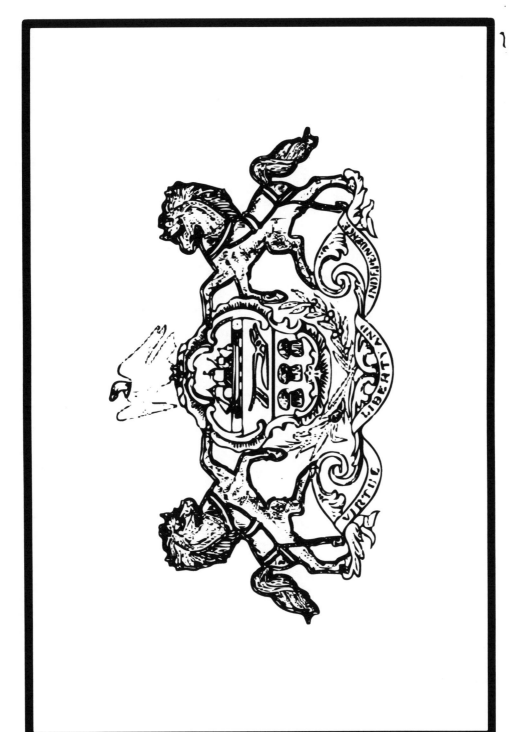

PENNSYLVANIA

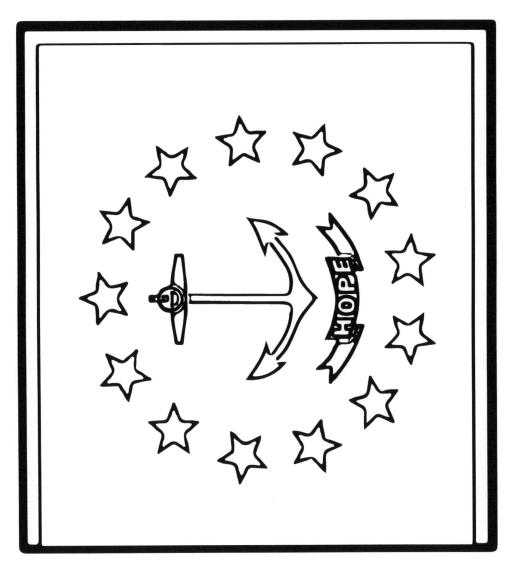

RHODE ISLAND

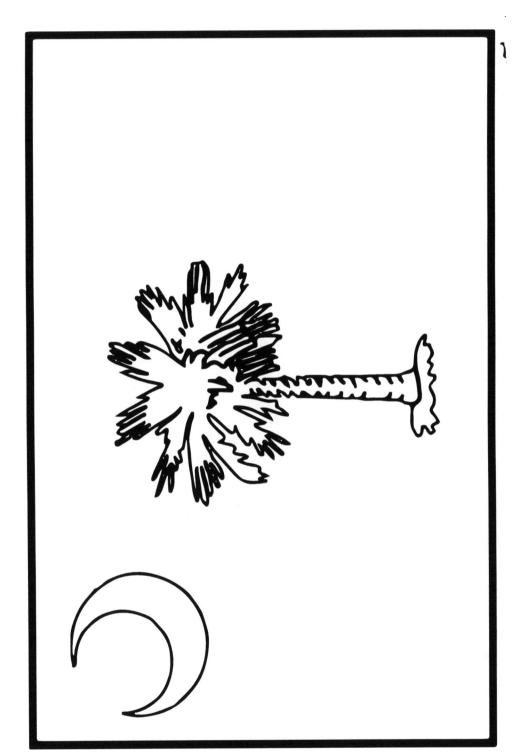

SOUTH CAROLINA

This is a Bleed Through Page If You Are Using a Coloring Marker or Pen!
Find Other Great Titles By searching for Kreativ Entspannen on Your Favorite Book Retailer
Amazon.Com | Barnes & Noble (BN.Com) | Books A Million (BAM.Com)

Kreativ Entspannen

COLORING / ACTIVITY BOOKS FOR ADULTS

SOUTH DAKOTA

TENNESSEE

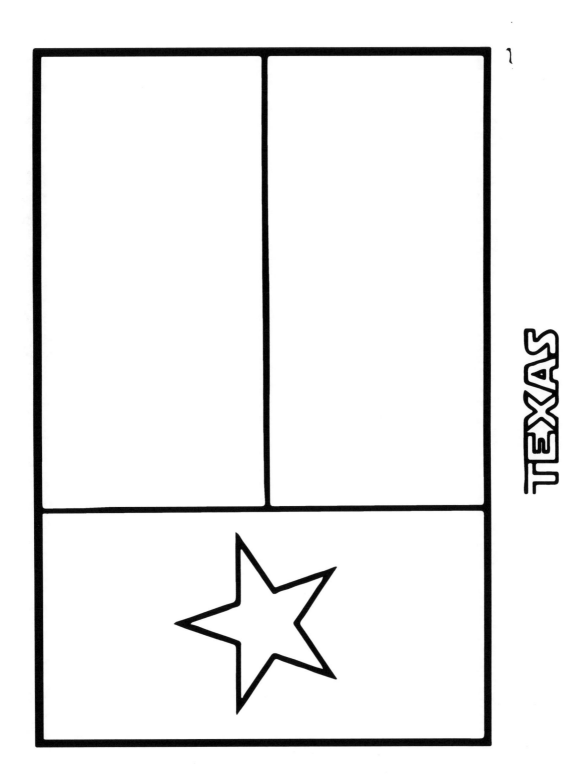

TEXAS

UTAH

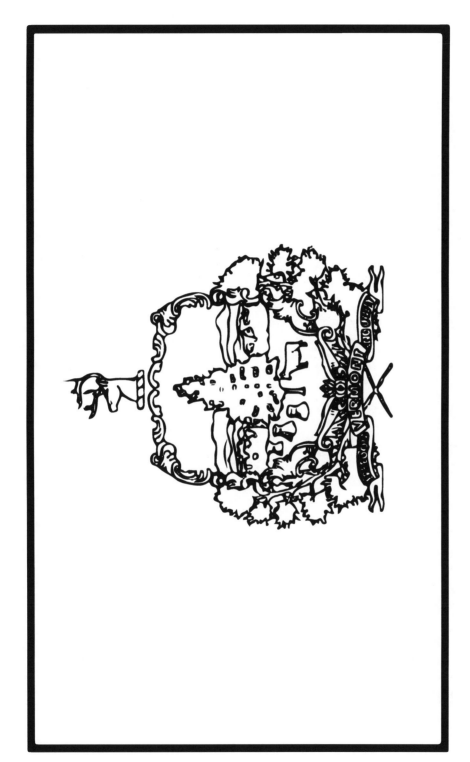

VERMONT

VIRGINIA

WASHINGTON

STATE OF WEST VIRGINIA

WEST VIRGINIA

WISCONSIN

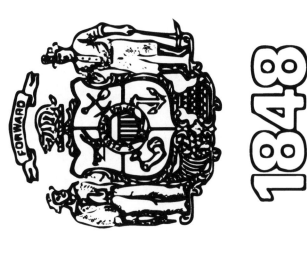

FORWARD

1848

WISCONSIN

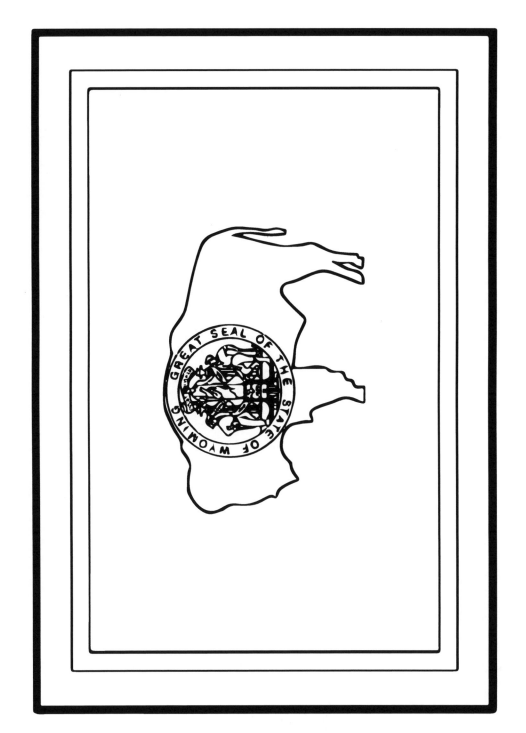

WYOMING

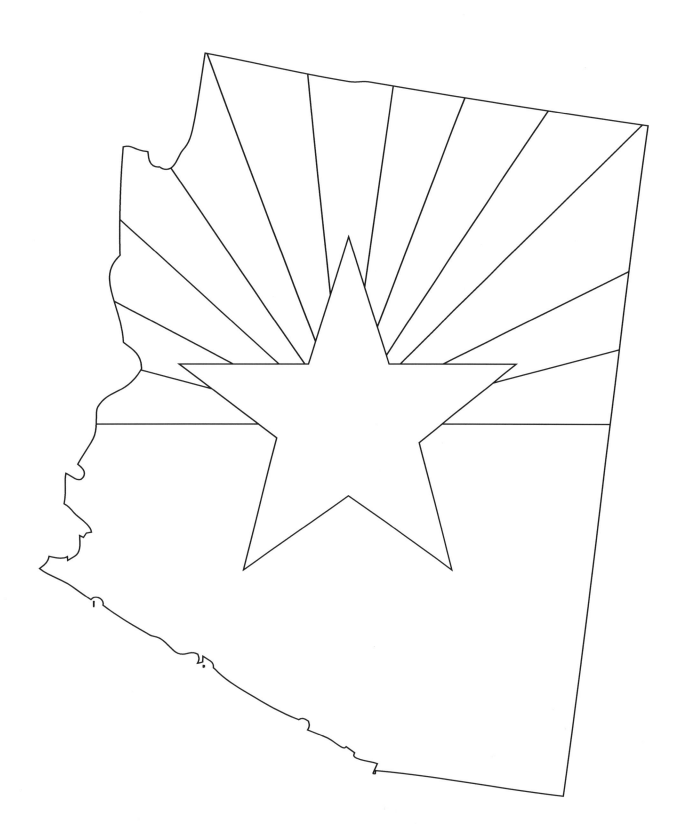

Made in the USA
Middletown, DE
07 March 2019